Death Valley

by Josie Martin

Harcourt
SCHOOL PUBLISHERS

Cover, p.14, ©PhotoDisc; p.4–5, p.12, ©Corel; p.5, (l) ©Corel, (r) ©Robert and Jean Pollock/Visuals Unlimited; p.6, ©O.S.F./Animals Animals; p.7, (b) ©Corel, (r) ©Patricio Robles Gil/Sierra Madre/Minden Pictures; p.8, (l) ©Corel, (c) ©Paul & JoyceBeriquist/Animals Animals; p.9, (r) ©Charles Melton/ Visuals Unlimited, (l) ©Corel; p.10–11, ©J. Emilio Flores/Corbis; p.11, ©Craig K. Lorenz/Photo Researchers, Inc.; p.13, ©Michael Andrews/Animals Animals.

Cartography, p.3, Joe LeMonnier

Printed in China

ISBN 10: 0-15-351539-2
ISBN 13: 978-0-15-351539-2

Ordering Options
ISBN 10: 0-15-351214-8 (Grade 4 Advanced Collection)
ISBN 13: 978-0-15-351214-8 (Grade 4 Advanced Collection)
ISBN 10: 0-15-358129-8 (package of 5)
ISBN 13: 978-0-15-358129-8 (package of 5)

4 5 6 7 8 9 10 0940 12 11 10 09

It's dawn in the desert known as Death Valley. The sun slowly creeps above the horizon, warming the vast area of land. As the hours pass, the temperature rises until it reaches over 100° Fahrenheit (37°C). The sun shines down on the sands that make up the desert. Death Valley is one of the hottest and driest places in the world. Death Valley is located in the northern part of the Mojave Desert in California.

You might think that such a hot, dry place would have no life, yet Death Valley is home to hundreds of plants and animals. All of these plants and animals have one thing in common. They have adapted to living in a hot, dry desert climate.

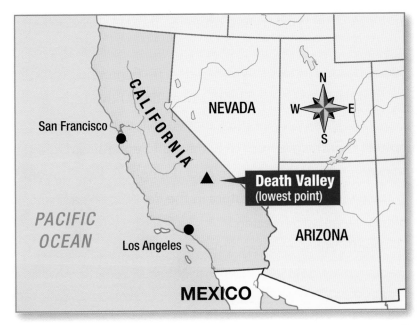

During the day in the desert, there is very little animal activity because the sun is simply too hot. As the sun rises in the sky, the temperature often reaches 114° Fahrenheit (45°C) during the summer. In fact, the hottest temperature ever recorded in Death Valley was 134° Fahrenheit (56°C)!

Surprising to some, Death Valley does have four seasons. There is a spring, summer, fall, and winter. The hottest months are from May through September. During the winter, temperatures are cool during the day. At night in the winter, the temperature in the desert can be chilly, but rarely gets to freezing.

Death Valley has very little water. In most years, Death Valley gets less than two inches of rain. So how do plants and animals survive?

You might know that plants need sunlight and water to live. Desert plants get plenty of sunlight, but most desert plants have adaptations that help them get water. One plant, the creosote bush, has very long roots that can reach water that flows far under the ground. The leaves of the creosote plant have a waxy coating. This keeps water inside the plant, preventing it from escaping through the leaves.

Cactus plants have adaptations that help them withstand the hot, dry heat, too. The roots of the cactus grow near the surface of the ground. After a rainfall, these roots are able to take in the water quickly and store it in the stem of the plant.

Plants are very helpful to the animals that live in the desert. During the day, insects hide in the leaves of bushes to get out of the hot sun. If you looked at the leaves of the creosote bush, you might notice a grasshopper or a cricket hiding.

Many desert animals are small. This makes it suitable for them to find shelter in bushes or under rocks. Insects and lizards may hide under rocks to keep out of the sun. Desert birds may perch in the shade of a bush or tree during the day.

Other animals hide from the hot sun by digging burrows, or tunnels, in the ground. One of these animals is the kangaroo rat. The burrow of the kangaroo rat is a cool place to sleep during the heat of the day. Foxes may sleep in a cool den, too.

Some desert animals have body parts that help them keep cool. A black-tailed jackrabbit has huge ears. The ears let heat escape from the rabbit's body when it is resting in a shady place. A desert owl may flutter its throat. This lets saliva come out of its mouth, allowing the owl to become cool.

Many desert animals get water from the plants that they eat. Bighorn sheep get water from cactus plants. They use their hooves and horns to extract the spines from the cactus. Then they eat the juicy insides of the plant.

When the sun is high in the sky, there is little activity in the desert. As the sun gets lower in the sky, the desert begins to come alive. At dusk, many animals come out of their hiding places. It is during this time that these animals hunt for food.

At dusk, a bird called a quail is ready for a meal. It eats fruits, berries, and seeds. A lizard comes out from under its rock to feed on leaves, buds, and flowers. A kangaroo rat also comes out of its burrow at night. It hunts for seeds that it will store in pouches in its cheeks. Then the rat will hide the seeds in small pits in the ground.

Some desert animals hunt other animals at night. Desert insects are food for animals such as birds, bats, and lizards. These animals get the water they need from the insects that they eat. A stealthy snake called a sidewinder comes out of its den. The snake gets water from the bodies of the animals it eats. One bird called the roadrunner is quick enough to catch a snake to eat. Like the sidewinder, the roadrunner gets its water from the animals it eats.

As the night passes in the desert, all of these animals hunt for food. When the sun rises at dawn, these animals go back to their dens and burrows with full bellies. There they sleep or rest until the night falls once again.

The changing seasons of the desert also affect how animals behave. Springtime in the desert is much cooler than the summer. In the cooler months of February, March, and April, the temperature rarely goes above 90° Fahrenheit (32°C). Most animals can live in a certain temperature range. When the temperature gets too high or too low, some animals may not be able to survive. Because of this, many desert animals begin to leave the desert at the end of spring when it becomes too hot for them.

Some birds will lay eggs in the early part of spring when it is cooler. Then they leave Death Valley at the end of the spring. The birds go to higher places, where the air is much cooler.

Some birds, such as the quail, stay in Death Valley all year long. The quail lays its eggs in March. About three weeks later, the eggs hatch. Soon the chicks will leave the nest to live in the desert on their own.

Another desert bird, the roadrunner, also lays its eggs in spring. Both male and female birds collect sticks for the nest. Then the female bird builds the nest in a bush, a cactus plant, or a small tree. Next, the female lays about two to twelve eggs. The eggs hatch in about three weeks. During the next two to three weeks, both parents care for the baby birds. Soon they too are ready to leave the nest to live in the hot, dry desert.

You might think that a desert is too hot and dry for
fish to live. There is one fish that is adapted to live in
Death Valley. This remarkable little fish is called the
pupfish. Pupfish are found in an area of Death Valley
called Salt Creek. There they live in shallow pools of
salt water. The water temperatures in the pools can get
up to 112° Fahrenheit (44°C). That's hot for a little fish.

In winter, however, the water becomes very cold in
the salt pools. During this time, the pupfish burrow into
the mud at the bottom of the pool. There they remain
until spring. Then the spring weather warms the water
in the pools. Soon the pupfish come out of the mud
and lay eggs.

Tiny pupfish hatch from the eggs as summer approaches. In the heat of the summer, the water in the pools dries up. Many of the pupfish do not survive. The pupfish that do survive go back into the mud when winter comes again.

Another animal that burrows in the mud during winter is the desert toad. Desert toads stay in the mud until the spring rains come. Then the ponds fill up with water. The toads come out of the mud and lay their eggs. Soon little toads hatch from the eggs and go off into the pond. They will burrow in the mud during winter. The cycle will repeat itself in the spring as the new toads come out of the mud to lay their eggs.

Death Valley sounds like a barren land, yet plants and animals can survive there. The cool night air gives all living things a rest from the heat of the day. The cycles of seasons make life possible. Animals give birth. Insect eggs hatch. Seeds become new plants.

All living things in the desert depend on one another to stay alive. Many animals, such as birds and lizards, eat insects and plants. Some of the smaller animals in turn become food for the larger birds and mammals that live in the desert environment. All of these plants and animals have adaptations that give them an advantage for surviving the hot, dry weather of Death Valley.

Think Critically

1. What adaptations does the creosote bush have that help it live in Death Valley?

2. How does the behavior of the animals in the desert change after night falls?

3. Why do some desert birds leave Death Valley when summer begins?

4. Why would a forest animal such as a deer or a squirrel not be able to live in Death Valley?

5. Would you like to visit Death Valley someday? Why or why not?

 Science

Desert Drawings How is the desert different during the day and at night? Draw two pictures of the desert, one of *day* and one of *night*. Add interesting captions to your drawings to explain what is happening.

School-Home Connection Ask family members what they picture in their minds when they hear the word *desert*. Then share some of the things about Death Valley that might change their "picture."

Word Count: 1,474 (1,488)